Endorsements

Receiving God's love is the foundation to the successful life you desire. His love removes fear, confusion, and insecurity and gives you confidence, direction, and purpose. *Love ANYWAY* shows you in a very practical way how to receive God's amazing, unconditional, and life-changing love.

—TERRI SAVELLE FOY is the founder and president of Terri Savelle Foy Ministries, which is making an impact in lives all over the world through media outreach, conferences, school projects, helping exploited women, France ministry, and more.

. . . .

In a culture full of false claims of promising happiness and satisfaction, the timeless truths found in *Love ANYWAY* shines the light on the path to real fulfillment. This book is an on-time message for the issues facing our world today. Well written, insightful and engaging!

—JEN TRINGALE is an internationally known speaker, author, and strategist on awakening destiny. She is known for her integration of purpose, innovation, faith, and spirituality. Her reach includes a robust international speaking schedule, her books *Your Defining Moment* and *Calling*, and a podcast that opened in iTunes' Top 40 charts with an audience of over 120,000 listeners in more than fifty nations. Jen is a graduate of Rhema Bible Training College, and is originally from Florence, KY. She embraces both her southern roots and Italian heritage, and now resides in Nashville, TN.

. . . .

We will all face a time in our lives when we are hurt or wounded. Then we are challenged to "Love anyway" so that we can move forward and heal. In my personal life I was facing a 17-year-old dead marriage that was loveless, hopeless and lifeless. But in one second both my husband and I decided if we were going to start all over and fall in love again with someone new then why not try to start over again from scratch in our own relationship. A miracle happened when we decided to "Love anyway"; 15-plus years later we are now happier and more in love than ever before.

You too can choose to "love anyway" as we unpack the applications that Adrienne walks us through to help build healthy relationship with those that you love the most. *Love ANYWAY* will certainly bring healing and wholeness to broken hearts and mend the most challenged relationships.

—LAINE LAWSON CRAFT is a funny and inspiring author, television host, speaker, and entrepreneur. Laine founded *WHOAwomen* and owned and published WHOAwomen magazine. Laine has authored two books, *Feeling God's Presence Today,* a 365-day daily devotional, and *Start Again from Scratch: A No-Fail Recipe to Revive Your Marriage,* and her new book *Enjoy Today Own Tomorrow* releases August 2020.

FOREWORD BY LISA YOUNG

Love ANYWAY

THE SECRET TO A HAPPY AND FULFILLED LIFE

FROM THE AUTHOR OF *HAPPY ANYWAY*

ADRIENNE COOLEY

WHERE DID ALL THIS *Love* COME FROM?

Where did all this love come from?

   Well, it sort of came from my mom Rebecca Spearman Massey. She was one of the sweetest people you could ever meet. It blows my mind that she wanted to be buried on a mountain in Oklahoma as to not make a big fuss over herself. That was her style. She was diagnosed with stage 4 lung cancer on a late night in November at the end of an otherwise typical day. By July of the following year we found ourselves saying our final good-byes. Even as the ink floods this paper, it's hard to believe these words. On that Alabama summer day, there was standing room only in the spacious sanctuary of our home church where my husband pastors. The day was filled with sentiments that remained constant from one person to the next. Even the cards that would follow for weeks echoed the same theme. Her loving nature was most remembered. She never held a microphone or sang from a stage but she led her family in worship during long drives from our country home to almost anywhere. No matter where we went, her warm smile and gentle countenance left those who encountered her better than before. She was clearly most remembered by her loving smile and loving ways, so it is only fitting to dedicate this book to her. Also, one of the most comforting things for me since she has been gone has been reading her words of wisdom in her many prayer journals. Her handwriting has soothed my soul. I love, love, love her handwriting and I hope you will too. A font has been made out of her handwriting so that her very touch is on this book.

Where did all this LOVE come from?

From a place of brokenness
From a place of being loved
From a place of loss
From a place of acceptance
From a place of pain
From a place of healing

IN LOVING MEMORY OF REBECCA SPEARMAN MASSEY

People are often unreasonable, illogical and self-centered;

Forgive Them Anyway

If you are kind, people may accuse you of selfish, ulterior motives;

Be Kind Anyway

If you are successful, you will win some false friends and some true enemies;

Succeed Anyway

If you are honest and frank, people may cheat you;

Be Honest And Frank Anyway

What you spend years building, someone could destroy overnight;

Build Anyway

If you find serenity and happiness, they may be jealous;

Be Happy Anyway

The good you do today, people will often forget tomorrow;

Do Good Anyway

Give the world the best you have, and it may never be enough;

Give The World The Best You've Got Anyway

You see, in the final analysis, it is between

You And Your God;

It has never been between you and them anyway.

Mother Teresa

Meet Larinda. She is so full of life and encouragement. She is a Godsend for me, and I couldn't imagine doing life without her. Her perspective is both authentic and profound, plus she is always loads of fun!

I'm thrilled that *Love ANYWAY* and its message is being published so I can share it with all my girlfriends who have had to listen to me talk about it for two years! I was blessed to be in a women's small group that the author, Pastor Adrienne Cooley, lead to test her ideas for *Love ANYWAY*. This was my 4th or 5th small group to participate in, and it totally stands out from the rest. Every meeting was like a free therapy session. Each one of us as members could relate to every chapter and each other. It didn't matter our age, marital status, or if we had kids or not. We can all grow and be our best selves from learning how to love anyway.

The common themes that I took the most from this book, and saved in my notes to refer back to, are:

1. Letting go of reconciliation is empowering and brings you to a place to love anyway.

2. We were made to connect. We are about as happy as our least happy relationships. The more connected we are to God, the more connected we are to ourselves.

3. The fruit of the Spirit is LOVE, JOY, PEACE, SELF CONTROL, PATIENCE. There is no circumstance in life that at least one fruit of the Spirit will not come to your aid and rescue you.

I know I speak for myself and all of my guests who attended this past year's Happy Girl Conference: We are ready and excited to dive deeper into learning how to enjoy the joy and love ourselves and others the way God loves us.

Larinda Gann

Harvest Church member, Happy Girl Conference attendee, and friend

Contents

Foreword: Lisa Young

. . . .

The gifts were prepared and ready for the precious pastors' wives accompanying me on a trip to Haiti.* They were a labor of love that I had made myself and was excited to share with the ladies. When I arrived at the gathering and began to unpack the gifts, they had been ruined in transit. What? All that work and now they were ruined. Well, what's a girl to do? I'm not one to cry over spilled milk or ruined craft projects so I just found a large trash bin and away they went! My new friend Adrienne was with me in the elevator on the journey to the bin. We just had to laugh as we admitted that the best plans we make often end up in a trash bin! Isn't it important to have friends to share the fun times and the hard times? Without a doubt Adrienne Cooley is that type of friend! It was that conversation that became a tiny seed, which helped grow Adrienne's first book *Happy ANYWAY*. Getting to know Adrienne has been a true gift. Her outlook on life is rooted in the relationship she has with Jesus, and it seeps into every aspect of her being. I've had the privilege of sharing time with this amazing friend and she truly "overflows" with the abundance that Jesus spoke of in John 10:10. Her purpose in writing is to help others experience this same abundance that is only found in Jesus.

With her new book, *Love ANYWAY*, Adrienne addresses a difficult principle for all of us to grasp, "to love and be loved." Actually, she redirects this popular cliché to its proper form, which is the foundation for transformational love. To "be loved and to love" is the order in which we find the secret to a lost love that the world so desperately needs and longs for deeply. Love is an overused word in our culture today and has been decaffeinated from its true meaning. In this book you will find the accurate picture of what love is all about and how to experience love in its truest form. How can we love others if we don't grasp the source of love and how it impacts our lives personally? It is only when we discover the "love source" that we can love the world as God intended. There are so many levels of love, and Adrienne

---

* In 2010, the devastating earthquake that ravaged Haiti orphaned millions of children. Our goal in Haiti was, and still is, to create a beautiful N.E.S.T. (Nutrition, Education, Sanitation, and Transformation) for those children living in such difficult circumstances. We are committed to bringing "love anyway" to these precious little ones!

breaks it down in a clear and meaningful way. What the world needs NOW is LOVE, sweet LOVE—found only in the author and creator of true love, Jesus!

• •••••••••••••••••••••••• ••••••

LISA YOUNG is the wife of Pastor Ed Young Jr. of Fellowship Church in Dallas, TX. Lisa communicates God's Word with warmth and grace, inspiring others to pursue a more intimate relationship with Him. Her passion is to see herself and others embrace the joys of walking with Christ in every day experiences.

Lisa is the founder of Flavour, a ministry designed specifically for women at Fellowship Church. Flavour was born out of Lisa's desire to show women their true value and worth in God's eyes and their potential to uniquely influence the world around them.

In addition to joining Ed on stage for special messages, Lisa is a gifted writer and has enjoyed co-authoring several books. Her most recent book is the *New York Times* bestseller *Sexperiment: 7 Days to Lasting Intimacy with Your Spouse*. Lisa's other contributions include: *The Marriage Mirror; The Creative Marriage; Beauty Full;* and *Kid CEO*.

In addition, she has written a cookbook, *A Dash of Flavour*, which offers simple, 'down-home' recipes that are healthy, filled with flavor and easy to prepare.

Lisa has a degree in Early Childhood Education. She enjoys cooking, nutrition, fitness, and spending time with Ed and their four children and grandchildren.

Introduction

This book was designed to be sort of like a favorite throw blanket to cuddle up with your favorite cup of coffee. My favorite books are ones I can make notes in, ponder questions that make me rethink some of my faulty belief systems, but aren't too complicated or deep. This book can be used as a private devotional, a small group curriculum, a book club, or even a discussion guide for a ladies conference!

I really hope you enjoy using the L.O.V.E. method with all the scriptures mentioned each week. Here is the gist of how it is supposed to work: On day one, simply read the lesson to get the week off to lots of love. On each day thereafter, dissect the verse. Dig in a little deeper by repeating the L.O.V.E. method. Every day offers a different Bible passage.

Here's the coolest part: I have designed this book to work for you on super busy days or on days when you plan to lounge in your pj's all morning with coffee in hand. On those rare days, you could dig in and spend an hour or so cross-referencing the verses, praying, journaling, and processing what God is speaking to you. So the L.O.V.E. method is a tool that can be used sort of like a hand spade on days you only have time to plant a couple quick "flowers" from the Word into the soil of your heart. But, when time allows, it can also be used like a hedge trimmer for more serious "gardening" when thought patterns and habits need to be pruned back into submission to Christ.

If you are anything like me, your days are NOT "One Size Fits All." And guess what? Neither are our quiet times with the Lord. Whether you are a 5 am-er or a night owl or somewhere in-between, this book can be a quick pick-me-up or could guide an hour-long devotion. My prayer is that you will find a group of friends and go through this book together. I believe God will show you through this study how to genuinely *Love ANYWAY* no matter what condition you find your relationships. This book was written from the place of a healed heart and my hope for you is that your heart will be healed too.

How to Use This Devotional

1. Read the week's chapter, and do a fun activity or get started on one L.O.V.E. method, picking out the verse that spoke to you most.

2. Simply repeat the L.O.V.E. method each day with a different verse from the week's chapter. Answer questions as you go along. Enjoy all the happy activities, quotes, and verses sprinkled throughout the book.

3. This study is not only about getting the spiritual side of things in order, there are also word searches and activities to engage your brain and so much more fun to be had!

4. If you really use this devotional the way it is intended, you will get out of it as much as YOU write in it, as I did. So enjoy it. Journal. Listen as God speaks to you and write it down!

5. Remember loving anyway doesn't mean everything is perfect, but it means you've decided to look beyond the imperfections. This book is going to help you do just that and strengthen the relationships that mean the most to you—imperfections and all!

...And Get The Most Out of it

I really hope you enjoy using the L.O.V.E. method with all the scriptures mentioned each week. Here is the gist of how it is supposed to work: On day one, simply read the lesson to get the week off to lots of love. On each day thereafter, dissect the verses you find in each chapter. Dig in a little deeper each day by repeating the L.O.V.E. method with each verse. The L stands for Love notes from Heaven or, in other words, a scripture from the current chapter you are reading. O is for Observation, so write your biggest "Aha" moment the Holy Spirit highlights to you. The V is sort of an action step (Love is a verb.) of how you Vow to be a doer of that Word. And E is for Examine your heart in prayer, then write out your prayer on the lines provided.

How this Fits Your Schedule

1. First thing, consider this: How badly do you need to figure out how to Love Anyway? How bad do family or friends need you to love them anyway? Let that desire drive you.

2. Find your happy place in your home, and keep your book there with your favorite pen. My comfy throw blankie is in my happy spot calling my name. It makes it more inviting to stop for some me-time, well, actually, God-time. God is love and being with LOVE is the biggest part of how to Love Anyway.

3. Your mind will fight you every step of the way, but you have to be determined not only to start but to finish, so you can truly learn how to be loved and to #loveANYWAY long term.

4. Find a friend to do this with so you two can talk about it together, and help each other along the way. This will make it so much more fun!

1. Congratulations for taking the plunge into learning how to Love Anyway!

2. Find a time and place to simply get together with a few friends. Text or call and invite them to join you for coffee or something super easy. Remember: Comfy and casual is the goal. No big fuss. Just make it a fun girl time! Also, consider spreading the happy by taking turns bringing snacks, if you choose to have them.

3. Engage a friend to help you keep everyone excited about finishing what God begins in each of your lives, and to assist you in encouraging everyone to see it through for the short six weeks.

4. Don't worry about feeling like you have to be qualified to teach or anything like that. All you have to do is facilitate lots of chatting—what we girls do best!

5. Be in charge, or recruit a "bossy" friend to help you keep the conversation going so one mouth-of-the-south doesn't dominate your time. Along those same lines, be sure to start on time and end on time. Less is more. Leave them wanting to come back for more, not dreading getting stuck all day.

6. If you do the L.O.V.E. method with four to five verses and answer the questions each week before you meet, you will be good to go come time to lead the group. It really only takes ten minutes a day (maybe more just for one or two days).

Meet my friend Jen Tringale who seemed like a sister from the first time we met. If you know her, she probably makes you feel that way, too. We adopted her as family right away. Love her so! And you are going to love her story.

The typical reasons people believe why happiness exists are a bit of a myth. That is why this book that you hold in your hand now will be a powerful tool in your life. In a world pointing us to success, status symbols, and popular opinion as the reasons for a happy life, we need a light to shine on the path to real joy. I remember such a time in my life.

The circumstances of my life had me in a tight place. I was in my early twenties, fresh out of college and working a full-time job at a local bank in HR. The dreams of my heart and the landscape of my reality were in complete contrast. My closest friends were seemingly living out their dreams, while I was struggling to make ends meet, spending my time at a job I didn't possess a passion for and living in isolation.

While driving to work one morning I prayed, "God, if I could just know everything will turn out alright...if I could see that where I am right now leads to where I dream to be, then I could handle this season and be happy."

And then, without any bravado, as simply as a wind blows gently across your face, these words came to my heart: "Although you can't see how your life is going to come together, what I Am offering you now is to look instead at My character. I Am faithful, I Am good and I only do good on your behalf. I Am with you and I Am preparing you for your future."

Suddenly, I realized I had every reason I needed to be happy in that season. His character, goodness, and His love were the reasons for my happiness.

It was a game-changer moment for me; one that has served me time and time again. When I began to trust in His love, life became more fulfilling. When circumstances didn't serve up reasons to be happy—I was already **Happy ANYWAY!**

Jen Tringale

1 WEEK
what's love got to do with it?

Love

"Ephesians 3:14-19 (NASB)

14 For this reason I bow my knees before the Father, **15** from whom every family in heaven and on earth derives its name, **16** that He would grant you, according to the riches of His glory, to be strengthened with power through His Spirit in the inner man, **17** so that Christ may dwell in your hearts through faith; and that you, being rooted and grounded in love, **18** may be able to comprehend with all the saints what is the breadth and length and height and depth, **19** and to know the love of Christ which surpasses knowledge, that you may be filled up to all the fullness of God. "

This passage is my go-to prayer for my family. I would like to begin this devotional with a prayer for you and me that we would know the breadth and length and height and depth of the love of Christ as we journey through *Love ANYWAY* together.

Father, I pray that You would strengthen us with might by Your Spirit in our inner man so that Christ would dwell in our hearts through faith. I pray that we would be rooted and grounded in love able to comprehend the vastness of Your love, that is beyond mere knowledge. My prayer is that we will be filled with understanding and filled with all the fullness of You, God!

I pray that this study will reveal the unfailing power of Your love in and through our lives. I declare by faith that each one who reads and applies Your Word presented in this study will live a life that cannot fail but instead is dominated by Your love. In Jesus' name. **So be it!**

THERE IS ONLY ONE
HAPPINESS IN LIFE...

TO LOVE
- AND -
BE LOVED!

First Corinthians 16:14 in the NLT says it best. It just cuts to the chase:

"And do **everything** with **love**."

Plain and simple. If we did everything in love, how different would this world look? How different would our lives be? I have good news! God wouldn't tell us to do something we can't do. We actually can live our lives in love. My hope is that this study is going to equip you to do just that!

Take a journey with me this week and let's search for real love and look at why things don't satisfy us the way we keep trying to get them to. Then, let's look into what love has to do with our search for a happy and satisfying life.

❝ 1 John 2:15 (NASB)

Do not love the world nor the things in the world. If anyone loves the world, the love of the Father is not in him. ❞

LIST A
Love songs
Romantic movies
Girlfriend getaways
First kiss
Coffee with a friend
Walks on the beach
Family game night
Children's play dates
Christmas Eve
Hallmark movies

LIST B
Shiny new car
Big house
Swimming pool
Country Club membership
Fancy vacations
Designer clothes
That updated kitchen
Expensive shoes
Dinner at high-end restaurants
Boats

Check out List A...
did you notice that none are tangible?

What do things in List A have in common? _____

What specific memories came to mind when reading this list? _____

_____

Think for a moment about the last time you got that coveted new car or dress. Did it feel amazing? How long did that feeling last? Now think of the last fun family dinner or that unexpected call from a friend? I'll bet that feeling lasted much longer.

Circle things in List B that you have and are thankful for, underline the things that you wish you had, and then cross out the things you don't want.

Note your thoughts... _____
_____
_____
_____

While it's perfectly fine to own every single item on List B, it's List A that makes our hearts go pitter-patter. With List A, my mind automatically plays a slide show of happy memories. But when I read List B, it's more like stock photos!

❝ 1 Corinthians 13:13 NLT

Three things will last forever—faith, hope, and love—and the greatest of these is love. ❞

I'll never forget watching a documentary of the most famous musician of the day. He was driving down the 101 realizing that at 25 he had reached the pinnacle of his career. "Now what? I'm really disappointed that this is it!" His later music centered on the themes of heartbreak and living without love.

The truth is we are all after the same thing, whether a famous musician in LA or a southern pastor's wife like me. No matter the country of origin, socioeconomic status, race, marital status, age, religion, or political persuasion, we all want to lead a happy, satisfying life. The question is WHAT'S LOVE GOT TO DO WITH IT? E V E R Y T H I N G !

Have you ever noticed...

LOVE is the essence of human experience and emotion.

It is at the ROOT of all and everything we do.

Without LOVE what do we have to live for?

Faith, Hope, and Love—

and the greatest of these is

Love.

1 Corinthians 13:13 NLT

“ Colossians 3:14-15 (NASB)

14 Beyond all these things put on love, which is the perfect bond of unity. **15** Let the peace of Christ rule in your hearts, to which indeed you were called in one body; and be thankful. ”

I love this! Above all these THINGS in our lives, love binds us to those we care about the most and produces the peace we all long for. This makes me think of the famous musician mentioned on page 13. No matter the level of success we reach or the amount of things we possess, we will eventually find out that what brings the most peace is love.

Can you think of a situation where you attempted to achieve peace through something besides love?

_____

_____

One translation of verse 14 says that love binds us together in agreement when each one seeks the best for others. We were made for connection and unity. That's why we are only as happy and fulfilled as we are connected.

Draw a dotted line between you and the ones you are praying for the breach in your relationship to be repaired. Circle the ones with whom your relationship is healthy and highlight the ones you feel God calling you to focus on in prayer and effort.

GOD
YOU

BOSS/EMPLOYEE   FAMILY   FRIEND   COWORKER

How could love be used to tighten the connections of your relationships?

_____

_____

Tip: Focus on your vertical connection with God and watch the horizontal connections thrive.

The Bible tells us that God is love. Harvard tells us, according to their 75-year-long Harvard Grant Study, that the secret to a happy life is love. It follows that God is Love is Happy. What's love got to do with it?

According to scientific research, love has EVERYTHING TO DO WITH IT!

#GodisLoveisHappy

WHO AM I & WHO DO I LOVE?

I'm _____

I love _____

_____

The best thing about my life is _____

_____

WHAT I DO THAT I LOVE TO DO

I love to _____

_____

3 3 REASONS WHY I LOVE THOSE THINGS

1. _____

2. _____

3. _____

*L*ove note from Heaven:

· ·

· ·

· ·

*O*bservation:

· ·

· ·

· ·

*V*ow:

· ·

· ·

· ·

*E*xamining my ♥ in prayer:

· ·

· ·

· ·

*L*ove note from Heaven:

....

....

....

*O*bservation:

....

....

....

*V*ow:

....

....

....

*E*xamining my ♥ in prayer:

....

....

....

*L*ove note from Heaven:

....

....

....

*O*bservation:

....

....

....

*V*ow:

....

....

....

*E*xamining my ♥ in prayer:

....

....

....

*L*ove note from Heaven:

....

....

....

*O*bservation:

....

....

....

*V*ow:

....

....

....

*E*xamining my ♥ in prayer:

....

....

....

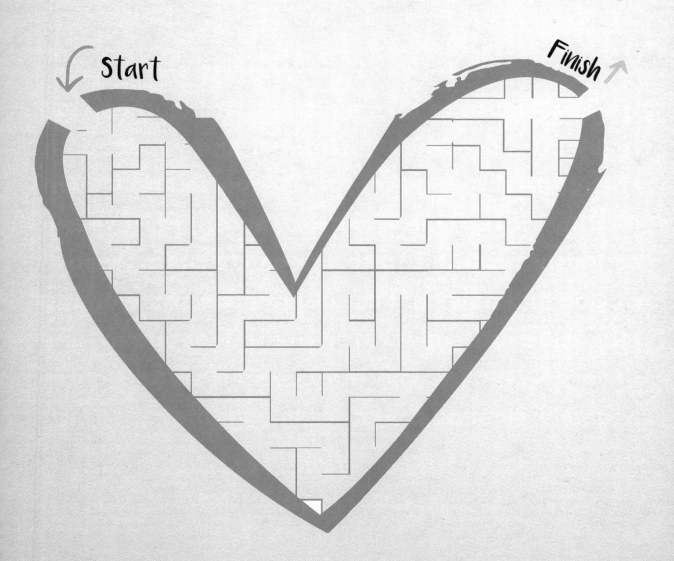

Start

Finish

Meet Ashley, who is such a bright light in my life and to anyone who meets her. Her hunger and growth in God is empowering to all around her including me.

It was because of this ministry that I learned God really does love me. I just didn't know that and it changed everything for me. Of course I had heard it all my life but when I chose to accept His love and seriously know this truth, I began to share the love of God and now I am in full-time ministry working alongside Adrienne! I'm so excited for you to read *Love ANYWAY* & join the Love ANYWAY Course and hear what all God does in your life!

—Ashley Weinacker

Harvest Church member, Happy Girl Conference attendee, and friend

2 WEEK he loves me?
he loves me not?

Love

He loves me. He loves me not.
He loves me. He loves me not.
He loves me.

This was my mantra in the fifth grade as I retreated to the back corner of the playground under the Mississippi pines during a hot, dusty recess. A small flower helped me discover the true feelings of a skinny, freckle-faced boy whom I named the cutest boy in fifth grade. On the days I was lucky enough for the last petal to tell me "He loves me," the little bit of confirmation helped me work up the courage to chase him relentlessly around the playground.

It's unfortunate that we seem to use a similar method in determining God's love at times. Life experiences may influence our abilities to receive God's love. Disaster, war, famine, violence, and tragedy come to bear, creating an uncertainty of a God who would allow such things.

These very questions were raised by my college philosophy teacher who spent the entire semester intellectually proving the existence of God. So it must follow that if we believe the truth of God's existence, we believe the truth of His Word.

"1 John 4:8b (NASB)
For God is love.**"**

"1 Corinthians 13:8a (NASB)
Love never fails.**"**

If A=B
and B=C
then it must be true that A=C
Philosophy 101

Let's apply the truth of these verses using this formula...

If God is love
and love never fails,
then it must be true that God will never fail us!

$$\dagger = \heartsuit = \cup^{||}$$

24

God will never fail us;
God **could never** fail us.
He is unable to violate His Word...
That's great news!
#TRUTH

But I can hear someone still thinking, "What about all the tragedy in the world? And in my life?"

15 "See, I have set before you today life and prosperity, and death and adversity. **19** ...choose life" (Deuteronomy30:15,19 NASB).

We may understand God gave us free choice. But we have to remember He also gave everyone else free choice. Some will choose to start wars. Some will choose to murder. Some will choose to drink and drive. God will not violate their free choice any more than He will violate ours. This is a harsh reality but true nonetheless. Yes, God is sovereign but His sovereignty doesn't override our will. I believe the secret things belong to the Lord and our finite minds are unable to fully understand the sovereignty of God versus free will. And that is the intersection at which we struggle to accept the things we face.

Journal what tragedy you wrestle with concerning God's love. Be honest. God can take it.

_____

_____

_____

Name a troubling situation in your life in which you carry a degree of responsibility due to poor choices.

_____

_____

We all could fill many lines answering the last question because as the motto of our church states: No perfect people allowed! Making some poor choices in life is inevitable due to our freedom of choice. Thank God for His mercy that works things out for our good! (See Romans 8:28.)

GOD IS LOVE
LOVE IS REAL

That means God is REAL!

Something I have noticed from observing friends and colleagues who have gone through massive tragedy, and what I have also found in my own experiences:

Those who trust God in the storm to turn things around for good and look for the silver lining, find it.

Those who sit down in the storm and let it overtake them, who choose to not fight back, stand up, or move to safety, or whatever the case may be, are overtaken by the storm.

Ask yourself...

Am I truly trusting God to turn _____ around for good?

Am I sitting down in the storm or doing my part to stand up like scripture admonishes us to do? "Having done all, to stand. Stand therefore..." (Ephesians 6:13,14).

What would standing up right now look like for me?

_____

_____

_____

_____

What would fighting back look like for me? (Example: Remembering what God's Word says about my situation instead of what it looks like.)

_____

_____

What would moving out of the storm to safety possibly look like for you? It could look like being in a good church surrounded by the right people. This happens by getting involved in the fabric of your church, serving in the body of Christ, being in a solid small group where you can be loved and held accountable, and moving beyond your situation as you listen to godly counsel. "In the multitude of counselors there is safety" (Proverbs 11:14).

" Isaiah 64:4 (NASB)

For from days of old they have not heard or perceived by ear, nor has the eye seen a God besides You, who acts on behalf of the one who waits for Him. "

In the moment of our despair, we may not see how He is working on our behalf. We may not even believe He is there at all. As a young girl, I was taken advantage of by a guy, I navigated through my brother's leukemia diagnosis as his bone marrow donor, and I later suffered through the untimely death of my mother. I too wondered where God was in these moments. Now as I look back on these events, I see God's benevolence in each one.

Concerning the tragedy you journaled about on the previous page, try to determine where God was in that moment. Ask Him to show you.

_____

_____

_____

_____

_____

I have made these same journal entries as you just did and have seen His healing power work things together for good as His Word promises. My prayer is that you will see His goodness working also, right in the middle of your situation. I pray you can open your eyes to His extravagant love for you!

"Consider the kind of extravagant love the Father has lavished on us..." (1 John 3:1 VOICE).

God proved His love to us by this...

"But God demonstrates His own love toward us in that while we were yet sinners, Christ died for us" (Romans 5:8 NASB).

Scriptures echo this truth in 1 John 4:9-10. Check this passage out in the NLT version!

CONSIDER
THE KIND OF
EXTRAVAGANT
LOVE
THE FATHER HAS
LAVISHED ON US.

1 JOHN 3:1 (VOICE)

"Deuteronomy 10:15 (NLT)

Yet the Lord chose your ancestors as the objects of his love. And he chose you, their descendants, above all other nations, as is evident today. "

This verse tells us that we are the object of God's love. There was a time we lived in Kolkata, India, and I became absolutely overwhelmed with all the human suffering and devastation around me. I couldn't see the truth of this verse and that led me down a slippery slope, doubting His very existence. Sunday School had taught me that God created us primarily to worship Him. With the vast poverty caving in on me, I was no longer able to reconcile that belief with what I saw surrounding me every day.

The question in my mind that had to be answered became clear. Why would I serve such an egotistical God? God, in His mercy didn't condemn me for having these questions. Instead He gently pointed me to the right question. Why did He create humanity in the first place? It was the words of my husband, Pastor Kevin Cooley, that settled this for me: "God did not create us to worship Him but rather to be the object of His kind benevolence."

This changed EVERYTHING for me! God wasn't an egotistical, full-of-Himself God after all. He created us to love us!!! His focus is loving us and so then the natural response is worship, adoration, and gratitude. Isn't that true in any relationship? This understanding set me free and I pray this truth transforms your perspective of God like it did for me.

"We love...because he loved us first" (1 John 4:19 NLT). He loved us from the very beginning whether we choose to love Him back or not.

Have you ever noticed...

God is so great at turning things around for the good
that sometimes He gets blamed for the storm.

God created man in His own image, in the image of God He created him; male and female He created them.

GENESIS 1:27 (NASB)

How cool is that?! God is love and He made us in His image, which means we were made to love and be loved by Him and each other. I pray that this understanding will help you really believe once and for all that He loves you—even more than our minds try to trick us that He loves us not!

He loves me/ Loves me not

Shade lightly in each petal that is true.
Color in with a dark color on each petal that is false.

He loves me.
He approves
of me.

He loves me.
He provides all
my needs.

He loves me not.
He caused my
sickness.

He loves me not.
He left me without.

He loves me.
He always causes
me to win.

He loves me.
He is my
strong tower.

He loves
me not.
He wasn't
there.

*L*ove note from Heaven:

....

....

....

*O*bservation:

....

....

....

*V*ow:

....

....

....

*E*xamining my ♥ in prayer:

....

....

....

*L*ove note from Heaven:

....

....

....

*O*bservation:

....

....

....

*V*ow:

....

....

....

*E*xamining my ♥ in prayer:

....

....

....

*L*ove note from Heaven:

· ·

· ·

· ·

*O*bservation:

· ·

· ·

· ·

*V*ow:

· ·

· ·

· ·

*E*xamining my ♥ in prayer:

· ·

· ·

· ·

*L*ove note from Heaven:

....

....

....

*O*bservation:

....

....

....

*V*ow:

....

....

....

*E*xamining my ♥ in prayer:

....

....

....

```
        F M V W            M B I I
      Z L T X P A        K E E C G F
      V Z I I P Z N N      J F M C B P Y G
    Q H S R A R Y K T I A Z O R C A L R B V
  B G A F U R P Z R M S M N D T G I N U S Q W
C A J P L R S M B T Y Y X J D R M Y V I F O S U
Y H S P I K I E B P Q R H X Y A H B Q W I C R O
K Y A Y I G S E J F M F A E F F A I T H E V O L
K S J B I Z O H N O O N M N A J M N L Y M X E B
G B Q K K H W D X D Y U N F O R G I V E J S T J
C W K V M E D L C W S Y K A I R T A C H Z H K J
  U Y Z G F G F A O P R G H A I H T E F Q B M
  G G M H I T Y N E Z P H M T C P R S C W Q Y
    S O O L G J C E R E H Q P R K U V S W A
    T P X P I D R V S B S A M R T Q Z X
      E Y S O K F O A K Y L V X H H W
      D D X R M A E E K J V S N B
        I Q Z X D R N H J D G Y
          O N H D N C G S J I
          G K G S G V D I
            D S M R A R
            U J I G
              D Q
```

WORD BANK

forgive	friends	heart	truth
anyway	family	God	faith
love	Heaven	real	hope
Jesus	prayer	happy	life

37

Meet Sasha. She was the first person ever to ask me to officiate her wedding instead of my husband. Such a sweet couple they are and I am so honored to get to have a front-row seat in their lives to watch God rock their worlds in the best kind of way.

Love ANYWAY impacted my life in ways I could have never imagined. Like a lot of women, I've had a hard time loving myself completely and forgiving myself (and others) for past sins and transgressions. Love *ANYWAY* and Adrienne helped me realize it is possible to both love and forgive myself! I recommend everyone complete the course, and get this book...it really makes all the difference!

−Sasha Thatcher

Harvest Church member, Happy Girl Conference attendee, and friend

3 WEEK

go ahead and love yourself

Love

Do you love you?

My hope is that by the end of this chapter
you will love you like never before!

So let's get a snapshot of before and see how it compares
to after this week. Think of this as a love note from you to you...

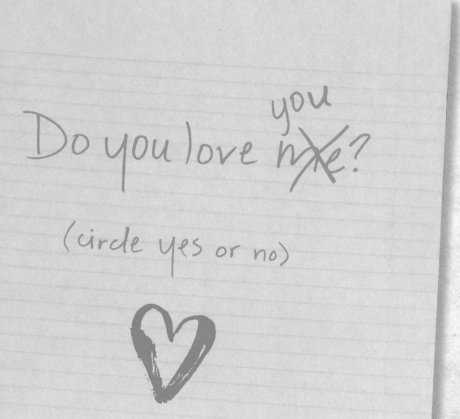

Do you love ~~me~~ you?

(circle yes or no)

#TRUTH

❝ Mark 12:30-31

30 'And you shall love the Lord your God with all your heart, with all your soul, with all your mind, and with all your strength.' This is the first commandment. **31** and the second, like it, is this: 'You shall love your neighbor as yourself.' There is no other commandment greater than these. ❞

This is a commandment, not a "this might be a good idea if ya wanna" suggestion.

Most of us in this Bible study are pretty good at verse 30, or we at least believe verse 30 and even the first part of verse 31. But it almost seems like no one has hardly even ever seen that second part of verse 31 or maybe we just haven't known what to do with it.

What I have learned in church my whole life is to put myself last. I've learned to sacrifice my all for others. I have learned that my needs don't matter. I've learned all that matters is to love God and love others. No one ever told me that the degree to which I will be able to love others is directly connected to the degree I love myself.

That is what this verse says. Re-read it for yourself. Look at that! What?!

Where has that verse been all my life?

The Message translation of verse 31 says it this way...

"Love others as well as you love yourself."

Think about it...You will only love others as well as you love YOU!

Is this concept new to you? What is God showing you right now through this amazing truth of just how much YOU matter?

41

Let's explore just what this Love looks like.

One thing it looks like for me is a whole lot more manicures!

More walks on the beach, which I love, more time on me and not just on everyone else. Can I get an AMEN?!

If you didn't think it were selfish, what are some things you would like to make a priority to do regularly for yourself that haven't been a priority?

(Draw a heart by all that apply)

Manicure

Massage

Exercise

Devotions Daily

Day Trips to the Beach

Tennis

Paint

Bubble Baths

Counseling

Read

Date Night

Cook More Creatively

Family Fun Nights

Lunch with a Friend

I LOVE skiing with family!

LOVE
yourself
like your life depends on it.

...because it does!

We are hardwired for connection and we see that in Mark 12:30-31.

We all have this deep need to love and be loved. We are social creatures and connection with each other is key for our well-being on every level.

"Happiness is not found in a what but in a who." —Pastor Joel Sims

First, happiness is found in God and then in others, but only in proportion to how happy we are with ourselves!

Have you ever noticed that you are typically as happy as your least happy relationship? Why is that? Because there are three types of relationships in which we must be strongly connected.

The first is with God, the second is with others, the third is with ourselves. If any of these relationship connections get loose, so do we! Do you see how our relationship with God affects our relationship with ourselves, and our relationship with ourselves affects our relationship with everyone else?

When our relationship with God is intact and we understand who we are in Him, then all of our relationships will be positively affected by that. I like to say it this way, if we keep our vertical relationship solid, all of our horizontal relationships will fall in line one way or the other.

This truth explains why no matter how many "whats" you have, they can never satisfy the lack of the "whos" that are most important to you. No amount of money, cars, houses, or diamond rings can substitute a life of meaning with people we love. That's because there is only so much connection we can have with stuff. Real connection is only enjoyed to its maximum potential between people and God.

Have you ever noticed...
you are typically as happy
as your least happy relationship?

44

When we are holding on to stuff behind us,
we cannot reach for the things in front of us.

Shame is the stuff we hide behind. Shame is the stuff we "should" all over ourselves and others. Regret is Shame's ugly cousin that keeps us tripping over things from our past. When we are holding on to stuff behind us, we cannot reach for the things in front of us.

Insecurity is the stuff that paralyzes us with fear of not-enoughness. Laziness is Insecurity's ugly cousin. It's the thought of "Why bother?" or "Who am I to think I can...?" When we reflect on the wrong questions, we never arrive at the answers we desperately are in search of that will propel us into the bright future God has for us.

So instead of "should-ing" all over yourself and getting hung up in the trap of "not-enoughness," let go of shame and regret, insecurity and laziness and join me in starting each day with a Daily Love Yourself Checklist! This is almost exactly like a paper that hung on my bathroom mirror to help me create self-loving habits. (You will see this checklist in a few pages. Tear it out and place it on your bathroom mirror as a daily reminder.)

Take action toward loving God, loving yourself, and loving others in a whole new way!

Shame grows in the dark and takes us over like a fungus. When we bring it out in the light in community, shame dies! So consider joining in a small group in your church where it is safe to discuss issues you face. Get involved in your church and let iron sharpen iron as scripture encourages. Be authentically and unapologetically you. Train people how to treat you. Take a step of faith and trust that God made you exactly how you need to be to accomplish the precise purpose He positioned you on this planet to accomplish.

How, you might ask, can I love myself when I know all the good, bad, and ugly about me?

1. Scripture tells us to look at ourselves through the mirror of the Word. When we are doers of the Word, we remember what we look like and who we really are. But when we forget who we are and the value that God has placed on us, it is because we are not continuing to see ourselves the way God sees us, and being doers of the Word. When we see ourselves the way He sees us, we will become who we are called to be and love who we are by recognizing our value! (See James 1:23-25.)

2. Scripture tells us how to think of ourselves. Romans 12:3 says not to think more highly of ourselves than we ought to but it does NOT say we should think poorly of ourselves. We, in fact, do need to think highly of ourselves, just not too highly of ourselves to the point of pride.

3. Scripture tells us that there is no condemnation for those who are in Christ (Romans 8:1). God's Word also says we are now reborn and renewed in Christ and old things are passed away, are no more, and no longer exist (2 Corinthians 5:17). If you are a Christian, you are no longer doing life in your own strength but in His! It's like rags to riches. It's like putting off old raggedy clothes and instead, now sporting the latest royal fashion! When you realize you are IN CHRIST, you walk in the room like you are the "best dressed," filled with confidence and awareness that you can do all things THROUGH CHRIST who strengthens you (Philippians 4:13). Take the pressure off yourself and realize it's all about the fact that you live and move and have your being IN HIM according to Acts 17:28.

NOTE:

Shame produces terrible self-talk. Seeing ourselves as God does, thinking highly of ourselves, and knowing who we are in Christ produces positive self-talk that will propel you into the life you always dreamed of!

Ok, let's get real...write down why you have a hard time loving yourself.

· ·

· ·

Now, let's be fair and write down what you like about yourself.

· ·

· ·

What can you change about these things or how can you capitalize on your strengths? Go ahead and put those items in your calendar so you can be proactive. Write the vision here and make it plain so you can run with it!

· ·

· ·

· ·

What can you not change that you need to ask God to help you accept?

· ·

· ·

Most of all, what does God's Word say about these things, and when you look into the mirror of God's Word, what do you see about yourself?

· ·

· ·

· ·

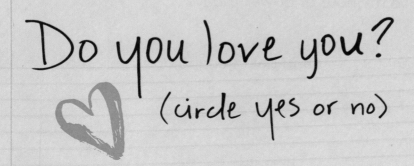

Do you love you?
(circle yes or no)

47

Daily Checklist

Tear this out and place on your bathroom mirror as a daily reminder!

☐ If I love myself, would I do what I am going to do today?

☐ Would Love say that?

☐ Who do I need to intentionally Love ANYWAY today?

☐ What will I do today to love God with all my heart, soul, and strength?

☐ Inventory worries and let Love Himself carry them instead of me.

☐ If I really love me, would I allow myself to experience...

☐ If this were my last day, would I do what I'm doing today?

☐ Did I have my hour of power today?

☐ Am I thankful, ⌣, and being unapologetically me?

† = ♡ = ☺

Love others

as well as you love yourself.

as well

—Mark 12:31 Message

49

Love note from Heaven:

....
....
....

Observation:

....
....
....

Vow:

....
....
....

Examining my ♥ in prayer:

....
....
....

$\mathcal{L}$ove note from Heaven:

....

....

....

$\mathcal{O}$bservation:

....

....

....

$\mathcal{V}$ow:

....

....

....

$\mathcal{E}$xamining my ♥ in prayer:

....

....

....

*L*ove note from Heaven:

....

....

....

*O*bservation:

....

....

....

*V*ow:

....

....

....

*E*xamining my ♥ in prayer:

....

....

....

*L*ove note from Heaven:

....

....

....

*O*bservation:

....

....

....

*V*ow:

....

....

....

*E*xamining my ♥ in prayer:

....

....

....

The Bible tells us that God is love (see 1 John 4:8). Science proves that Love is happy.

The Harvard Grant Study, a 75-year-long study costing 20 million dollars, revealed that the secret to a happy life is love. Dr. George Vaillant concluded that there are two pillars of happiness. He put it this way, "One is love. The other is finding a way of coping with life that does not push love away." He goes on to say the study points to "a straightforward five-word conclusion:

'Happiness is love. Full stop.'"

So based on simple logic, I have concluded that...

God is Love is Happy!!

1. What color is your love?
   - A. Red
   - B. Pink
   - C. Yellow
   - D. Purple

Find Your
LOVE TYPE

2. Romanticize—would you rather:
   - A. Fancy restaurant
   - B. Ride in the country
   - C. Picnic
   - D. Movie

3. What is the driving force behind your love?
   - A. Connection
   - B. Serving others
   - C. Happiness
   - D. Doing what's right

4. What is the most important qualities you look for in a BFF?
   - A. Energy
   - B. Easygoing
   - C. Funny
   - D. Loyal

5. Date night! Quick, pick a lipstick...
   - A. Deep Rose
   - B. Favorite Neutral
   - C. Gloss with a Hint of Color
   - D. Trending New Color

6. You, friends, and the open road...
   - A. Interstate all the way
   - B. Familiar Back Roads
   - C. Any road—as long as we have a GPS
   - D. City cut throughs

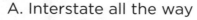

· ·

ANSWERS (NO PEEKING!)

Mostly A's—Passionate: You love hard but need to be sure to guard your heart.
Mostly B's—Gentle: You love generously but need to be sure to love YOU, too.
Mostly C's—Sunny: Your love is spontaneous but you need to make sure it is also consistent.
Mostly D's—Spunky: Your love is adventurous but you need to be sure others can keep up with you.

Lovers

GONNA

love

XOXO

I'll never forget the first day I met Heather. She was speaking at a women's event and I was that girl who went up to talk to her afterward in tears. I was a total mess. She so graciously has befriended me and continues to inspire me maybe more than any other to be unapologetically me. Her blogs have been a source of strength to me for years now. To know her is to love her.

A few years ago, my eight-year-old's dentist appointment had him trembling, wincing, clutching and resisting, as they pulled a tooth without any numbing. I will never forget that day for Andy, but I also can't forget his older brother DJ. There was finally a point during the procedure when DJ couldn't take Andy's pain anymore. So he turned the stool he was sitting on and faced the corner. Sometimes love has to look away. There's a heart-wrenching moment in the Bible when Jesus was on the cross and cried out to God, "Why did You forsake Me?" I am not a biblical scholar but I would surmise that Jesus felt like God looked away. And maybe, as Jesus took on all the sin of the world, God did. But nobody loved Jesus more than God. But sometimes, instead love has to look away.

I've watched good, godly parents turn in their addicted, suicidal and even criminal children. As the authorities took their child away—in their undeniable love—they looked away. We can love others so much that to look at them in their suffering or struggle can render us useless. But to hold on to them and keep looking at them might prevent the best from happening. God the Father had to let His Son die on the cross. I had to let Andy's tooth be pulled. Sometimes love has to look away. But for Jesus, it took Him from a cross on Earth, to a throne in Heaven—and you and me from our wretched sinful lives, to eternal forgiveness and freedom. Love does that.

Heather Palacios

Heather is married to Raul Palacios and they have two sons, DJ and Andy. Raul and Heather are on staff at Church by the Glades. Heather is a graduate of Judson University, where she received a BA in Business Management. Heather is also founder of "WondHerful," a mission dedicated to mental health and suicide extinction through blog posts (https://wondherful.com), social media posts (@WondHerful), and an eclectic speaking circuit that includes churches, businesses, prisons, police stations, schools, halfway houses, psychiatric wards. Heather is a suicide survivor and a diagnosed bipolar who believes that if you wake up breathing, that's your proof to keep going!

WEEK 4

love you,
love you more,
love you most!

Love

59

Love you, Love you more, Love you MOST!

Twenty one, newly married. Tulsa, Oklahoma, 41st and Garnett. One bedroom apartment, fewer square feet than our current back patio. Dried roses on the wall for decorations. Shake and Bake for dinner. Arguing over who loves whom the most...

Those were the days. Those were the moments we literally were living on love and a few bucks. Can you remember a time arguing over who loves who the most? Sweet memories.

Back to now. That was a nice trip down memory lane. Hope it took you back to a happy place, too! Maybe this is a version of your now. Yay, you, if so!

Let's get real though. We don't tend to live here all the time. Sometimes it looks more like this:

Thirty-two, thirteen or wherever you are on life's road; married, divorced, or dreaming of that hopeful day; pinning your dream house on Pinterest; packing up what's left of a broken dream; fine dining instead of peace and quiet; go-go-go; arguing over whatever the conversation is about; just nothing but arguing, pain, relational unrest, betrayal, and wondering who the next hater will be.

Wow, that went from Heaven to hell in a matter of three minutes, just like life does at times, right?!

The roller coaster of life we all know well. How do we stay balanced when it no longer is a mystery who loves most and who loves no more?

Have you ever had someone who chose to stop loving you more or most and just up and left your life? You clearly are the one left loving most while they love no more. Or if they do, they sure have a funny way of showing it! What to do?

Here's what I did to sort through things like that—and it was very healing. I double-dog dare you to try it. It takes bravery though. I will warn you!

- Get a pen and a piece of notebook paper and draw a line down the middle of the paper. Write the word "Haters" at the top of the left column and "Lovers" at the top of the right column.
- Go for it! Face it. Write down the names in the left column of people you feel have deserted you, hurt you, betrayed you. They may not

actually "hate" you, but in the spirit of Taylor Swift, they fall in that category.

- Now, in the right column, write down everyone you enjoy. They enjoy you. These are people you do life with and you know they have your back. These are also people who casually "love" you and you wish you knew them more. They probably wish they knew you more. You could see getting to know them better.

Note: Some family will fall in each column most likely. Friends will land in the right category and frenemies will land to the left. Tears might be shed as you write down the real and the raw.

HATERS: LOVERS

Once it is in black and white, sit back and accept it as it is. This is key. Then give it to God and ask Him to help you process it. Both the loss and the love. Feel the relief. I hope your list will prove to be like mine. I felt like the Hater list was going to be sooooo long. In my mind, it was. But on paper it was super short. The list of Lovers flowed over pages. Love welled up in my heart and I made a choice right then to focus my eyes ONLY on the right side of the page. Pick a person or two from the right side of the paper to invest in over the coming weeks. Call them, text them. Reach out and make a coffee date with them. Focus on who IS in your life instead of who is NOT.

Glance over the left side thanking God for bringing them into your life and for what you gleaned, remember the good times and forget the bad. People say to pray for them and yes, the Bible also says to and you should. I did and do but no-where near as much as I used to, and nowhere near as much as I do for the list on the right side of the page. Over time the first list that flowed from your pen onto that paper so effortlessly will matter less and less. The people won't matter less, but the hurt and pain associated with their names will fade into the distance and the joy related to the second list will become front and center in your life.

XOXO

LOVE

is when the other person's

HAPPINESS

is more important **than your own.**

Before long you will find yourself enjoying the people in your life and hardly bothered by your haters. You will find yourself saying, "Love you. Love you more. Love you most" to those who playfully say it back to you. You will find yourself in healthy relationships trying to out-love each other.

brutiful

[br(utal) + (beauti)ful]

THIS WORD INVENTED BY ED YOUNG JR.

"Faithful are the wounds of a friend..." (Proverbs 27:6)

Life is brutal. One of the main reasons is because of how true Proverbs 27:6 is. That's the most brutal part.

"Love from the center of who you are; don't fake it." (Romans 12:9 MSG)

"Be kindly affectionate to one another with [sisterly] love, in honor giving preference to one another." (Romans 12:10)

And that is the most beautiful part! Isn't it wonderful when there is honor and kind affection shared between us and those we love?!

"But love your enemies, do good, and lend, hoping for nothing in return; and your reward will be great, and you will be sons of the Most High. For He is kind to the unthankful and evil." (Luke 6:35)

Acceptance is a huge part of loving your enemies. The cliche "It is what it is" has become more real to me recently. I think I understand why that became such a popular saying. It is powerful when we accept things we cannot change and simply say, "It is what it is." It's great when we have the faith or ability to change things, but when things are out of our control, sometimes the healthiest thing to do is say, "It is what it is." For me, acceptance of the decisions of others has helped me to love them anyway and keep moving ahead.

I've learned to accept that sometimes I am going to be the one who loves more and most likely, there will be times when others will love me more. The more we try to out-love God, even though it's impossible to do, the more we will make it our aim to out-love others and get back into the silly "I love you. I love you more. I love you most" exchanges!

Acceptance
IS A
HUGE
PART OF LOVING YOUR ENEMIES

love,
from the
center of
who you
are,

don't
fake
it!

ROMANS 12:9 (MSG)

Love week CHALLENGE

- [ ] **Day 1:** Assume positive intent.

- [ ] **Day 2:** Speak with a kind tone only.

- [ ] **Day 3:** Write an encouraging note.

- [ ] **Day 4:** Surprise someone you love with a happy.

- [ ] **Day 5:** Do something extra helpful for a friend.

- [ ] **Day 6:** Treat yourself to a spa day or something you love.

- [ ] **Day 7:** Express thankfulness to your family.

Feeling adventurous?
GO FOR THE GOLD AND TRY TWO WEEKS!

*L*ove note from Heaven:

....

....

....

*O*bservation:

....

....

....

*V*ow:

....

....

....

*E*xamining my ♥ in prayer:

....

....

....

*L*ove note from Heaven:

....

....

....

*O*bservation:

....

....

....

*V*ow:

....

....

....

*E*xamining my ♥ in prayer:

....

....

....

*L*ove note from Heaven:

· ·

· ·

· ·

*O*bservation:

· ·

· ·

· ·

*V*ow:

· ·

· ·

· ·

*E*xamining my ♥ in prayer:

· ·

· ·

· ·

*L*ove note from Heaven:

· ·

· ·

· ·

*O*bservation:

· ·

· ·

· ·

*V*ow:

· ·

· ·

· ·

*E*xamining my ♥ in prayer:

· ·

· ·

· ·

DRAW...

Who **God** is to you	What **love** is to you	What **happiness** is to you

#GodisLoveisHappy

This story from my dear friend Laine is the perfect example of what it looks like to forgive anyway. What God did for Laine and her family, He can and wants to do for you and yours! Her powerful testimony will encourage you that God is The Way Maker even in your most hopeless and desperate hour.

When Steve and I got married thirty-two plus years ago, we never dreamed our first seventeen years would become hell on earth. We were living on opposite ends of the house and resenting one another greater every day. We knew we were doomed for divorce. But God had another plan.

Steve and I realized after going to counseling that our marriage was over and dead. But we had a revelation inspired by God. In a single instant, years of arguments, mistrust, broken promises and wounds were erased. We decided that if we were going to divorce and start all over again with someone else why not ask God to move miraculously and help us to confess then forgive one another and start again from scratch with each other. Forgiveness was the "key" to activating the miraculous power of God to move to us and through us.

Basically, when we decided to "Love Anyway" and lean into God's ways and God's miraculous power then we could find a way to love one another again. Confession from both of us and offering forgiveness from both of us is what instantly brought resurrection to our dead marriage. We brought love back to our marriage through the power of forgiveness and our relationship became whole again. We were transformed by the power of God as He equipped us to forgive and to "Love Anyway," so that we could live happier and more in love than we could ever dream or imagine.

Laine Lawson Craft

Laine Lawson Craft is a funny and inspiring author, television host, speaker, and entrepreneur. Laine founded WHOAwomen and owned and published *WHOAwomen* magazine. Laine has authored two books, *Feeling God's Presence Today, a 365-day daily devotional,* and *Start Again from Scratch: A No-Fail Recipe to Revive Your Marriage,* and her new book *Enjoy Today Own Tomorrow* releases August 2020.

5 WEEK

forgive anyway

Love

forgive

forgave for \fər-'gāv, for-\;
forgiven for \fər-'gi-vən, for-\;
forgiving

transitive verb

1 to cease to feel resentment against (an offender): pardon//
forgive one's enemies

2 a: to give up...requital for //forgive an insult **b:** to grant relief
from payment of //forgive a debt

The Greek word translated forgiveness in the Bible
literally means "to let go."

❝Isaiah 43:25-26 MSG

25 But I, yes I, am the one who takes care of your
sins—that's what I do. I don't keep a list of your sins.
26 So, make your case against me. Let's have this
out. Make your arguments. Prove you're in the right.❞

When forgiveness comes easy...

Forgiveness will come easier when we can talk it over with someone and clear the air. Can you think of a time when forgiveness was given or received because you were able to talk through the matter?

_____

_____

What about a time when one or both parties were not willing to talk it out?

_____

_____

Acts 3:19 (NASB)

"Therefore repent and return, so that your sins may be wiped away, in order that times of refreshing may come from the presence of the Lord."

When someone comes and repents in humility, turning back toward you, it's easy to forgive quickly. Much like the times of refreshing that follow God forgiving us, there is then a sweet refreshing in that relationship. This is especially true when the offender returns willingly and doesn't need to be chased, with little to no reciprocation.

In which relationship do you need to experience times of refreshing as a result of forgiveness?

_____

_____

Isaiah 1:18 (NASB)

"Come now, and let us reason together," says the Lord, "though your sins are as scarlet, they will be as white as snow; though they are red like crimson they will be like wool."

The first to apologize
is the bravest.

The first to forgive
is the strongest..

The first to forget
is the happiest.

Oh, isn't forgiveness so much easier when everyone is reasonable about what happened.

Could you be more reasonable in any current situation in order to reach a solution with a friend or family member? Explain:

_____

_____

_____

(Tip—It's easier to see the speck in their eye than the plank in our own, so ask God to show you where you could perhaps be more reasonable.)

" Luke 17:3-4 (NASB)

3 Be on your guard! If your brother sins, rebuke him; and if he repents, forgive him. **4** And if he sins against you seven times a day, and returns to you seven times, saying, "I repent," forgive him. "

Though a workable scenario, it may be exhausting to forgive over and over. We see where boundaries are encouraged, as in an "open customer service counter." This means safety to discuss grievances in a gracious way with the knowledge that forgiveness will be granted in both directions. This type of healthy relationship is typically with closer friends and family.

Which relationships in your life have an "open customer service counter"?

_____

_____

"1 John 1:9 (NASB)

If we confess our sins, He is faithful and righteous to forgive us our sins and to cleanse us from all unrighteousness. "

This is an ideal picture of a healthy relationship between us and God, and us and others. When we confess, He forgives. It can be just that easy but not always.

When forgiveness

❝ Ephesians 4:31-32 (NASB)

31 Let all bitterness and wrath and anger and clamor and slander be put away from you, along with all malice. **32** Be kind to one another, tender-hearted, forgiving each other, just as God in Christ also has forgiven you. ❞

Remember, the Bible definition for forgiveness is "to let go." When we let go of bitterness and its friends, we make room for kindness and a tender heart. This is fertile ground for forgiveness!

We probably all hold on to bitterness in some area or have in the past. Ask God to reveal bitterness in those areas. Ask God to reveal bitterness you may not even be aware that is still lurking deep in your heart.

_____

_____

_____

❝ 2 Corinthians 5:17 (NASB)

Therefore if anyone is in Christ, he is a new creature; the old things passed away; behold, new things have come. ❞

When people are in our lives, we can walk in unity. Even if we have a rocky past, relationships that are in Christ are new and the old things no longer matter. It doesn't mean that there was not a legitimate need for forgiveness. It just means that when we walk with our eyes fixed on Christ, we can let all offense go.

What relationship in your life may have formerly been troubled but has now been made new in Christ? How did that happen?

_____

_____

_____

❝Daniel 9:9 (NASB)

To the Lord our God belong compassion and forgiveness, for we have rebelled against Him.❞

❝Romans 12:21 (NASB)

Do not be overcome by evil, but overcome evil with good.❞

There are those times when people rebel against us or choose not to repent. This doesn't get us off the hook of forgiveness. Just as God forgave us in our rebellion, we have to do good and forgive anyway. I've heard it said that forgiveness is setting someone free and finding out that someone is you. Tell of a time when you rebelled against God and He in His great compassion overcame your evil with good.

_____

_____

_____

In what way can you overcome evil with good in your life?

_____

_____

_____

"Our Father who art in Heaven, hallowed be thy name. Thy kingdom come, thy will be done, on earth as it is in Heaven. Give us this day our daily bread; and **forgive us our trespasses, as we forgive those who trespass against us;** and lead us not into temptation, but deliver us from evil. For yours is the glory and power forever and ever, **amen.**"

Matthew 6:9-13 (RSV-2CE)

The goal of Forgiveness is not: To reconcile the relationship.

* Although you may pray for this, there is another person's choice involved. If you set this as a goal, it can be very frustrating when you discover your lack of control. Forgiveness can be achieved in your own heart regardless of reconciliation.

* Sometimes we build images in our minds of an imagined future or treasured past in an estranged relationship. An open heart allows us to be ready for a new reality God can create.

* Forgiveness is not an immediate relief from the pain. But it is the first step in working through the emotional trauma of loss. God will use it in the healing process.

The goal of Forgiveness is: To cleanse your own heart which strengthens your connection with God.

Psalm 103:12 (NASB)

"As far as the east is from the west, so far has He removed our transgressions from us."

Are we able to remove people's transgressions as far as the east is from the west? We are made in His image, so we have the capability. Let's trust God together to be able to walk that free of unforgiveness!!

Psalm 86:5 (NASB)

"For You, Lord, are good, and ready to forgive, and abundant in lovingkindness to all who call upon You."

God does not want us to portion out forgiveness in teaspoons but in bucketfuls. If we are Christlike, we will be abundant in lovingkindness, ready to forgive at the drop of a hat.

THINK ABOUT IT!

WHICH COGNITIVE DISTORTIONS ARE GETTING IN YOUR WAY OF FORGIVENESS AND LOVE?

Irrational thoughts can influence your feelings. We all have cognitive distortions to some extent; however, when these thoughts are taken to the extreme, they can be harmful. Try focusing on just one distortion per week, catching yourself in the act. Practice stopping those thoughts and replacing them with what scripture says about you and others.
Enjoy healing in your relationships as you experience this change.

Circle the ones that you struggle with and ask God to help you renew your mind as you search the scriptures. You will find that these cognitive distortions will have less and less hold on your mind as you replace these habits with habits found in 1 Corinthians 13!

MAGNIFICATION/MINIMIZATION Over/under exaggerating the importance of something. Example: I have a few accomplishments under my belt, but nothing that's really impressive." "My mistakes are so stupid. Nobody but me would ever do anything that dumb."

OVERGENERALIZATION Viewing a single/few negative event(s) as a pattern of never-ending defeat. Example: "I was so awkward at that party. I will always be awkward at parties."

CONCLUSION JUMPING Interpretation with little to no evidence. Example: "She will never give me the job. She probably thinks I'm untalented." "I just know I'm never going to get that job."

EMOTIONAL REASONING You assume that your feelings are an accurate depiction of how things really are. Example: "I feel like a bad Mom; therefore, I must really be a bad Mom."

PERSONALIZATION You believe that you're responsible for events over which you have no control. "My partner is always angry. If only I could do more to make him/her happy..."

"SHOULD" STATEMENTS Believing that things must be a certain way. Example: "I should always be perfect."

ALL-OR-NOTHING THINKING Using absolutes. Example: "You ALWAYS do this. You NEVER think about me."

DISCOUNTING POSITIVES Allowing the negative aspects to overshadow the positive. Example: "That one B on his report card is unacceptable!"

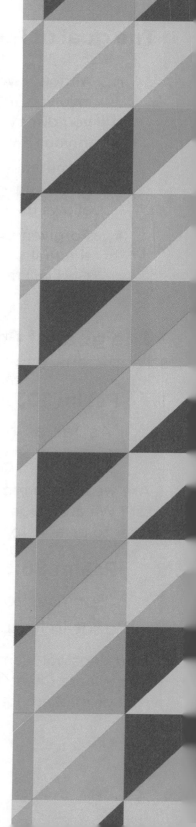

*L*ove note from Heaven:

....

....

....

*O*bservation:

....

....

....

*V*ow:

....

....

....

*E*xamining my ♥ in prayer:

....

....

....

*L*ove note from Heaven:

....

....

....

*O*bservation:

....

....

....

*V*ow:

....

....

....

*E*xamining my ♥ in prayer:

....

....

....

*L*ove note from Heaven:

....

....

....

*O*bservation:

....

....

....

*V*ow:

....

....

....

*E*xamining my ♥ in prayer:

....

....

....

*L*ove note from Heaven:

....

....

....

*O*bservation:

....

....

....

*V*ow:

....

....

....

*E*xamining my ♥ in prayer:

....

....

....

How many words can you make out of

LOVE ANYWAY?

Cheryl is a friend who has inspired me and many others to be brave and go for it! You are going to fall in love with her style, her products, and her! I'm so proud of her accomplishments and that she calls me friend.

In a time when modern culture is fixated on differences, labels, and judgments, the concept of *Love Anyway* is a powerful alternative.

What should we do when our society is pushing toward an era of separateness and isolation for those we do not agree with? *Love Anyway* is the answer. Of course, there are times when walking away from toxic people and situations is a must. But I hope that comes after much thought and consideration and not because it feels easier to just walk away.

There are so many relationships worth saving. Some people in our lives need a little extra grace. Most of us have been gifted with someone who challenges our idea of love and acceptance. Yes, they too are a gift. They help us grow in our capacity and our patience. After all, we are called to love, and not only when it is easy or convenient to do so.

WHAT DOES IT TAKE TO *LOVE ANYWAY?*

Bravery. Yes, that's right. Be brave enough to be vulnerable and bold enough to love when it would be much easier to turn away.

WHAT DOES IT LOOK LIKE TO *LOVE ANYWAY?*

Loving anyway is not about being a doormat or taking abuse. Loving anyway sets boundaries but it is not deterred by uncertainty and difficult days. Love perseveres. Love stands when everything else is falling apart. Love does not try to prove its own "rightness." Love covers a multitude of sins.

It is the grace we hope to receive for ourselves when we are the ones in need.

So, dear girl, be brave, be bold and love anyway.

Cheryl Hale

Cheryl Hale is the author of *Girl Be Brave: 100 Days to Chart Your Course* and the founder of the Girl Be Brave movement. To learn more about this brand with purpose, visit her site at www.girlbebrave.com.

88

How many times a day do you find yourself needing to *Love Anyway?* Here's what comes to mind...

*   When the nail tech cuts your cuticle as she files your nails and inflicts just enough pain to be irritating for days to come. Really?!

*   When your son forgets to take out the trash. Yucky, stinky trash! Now what to do until next week's trash day?

*   When your husband doesn't do exactly what you want him to do AGAIN.

*   When the lady in the grocery store was rude. What did we do to get the brunt of her life spilled all over us in the cereal aisle?

*   When the guy wouldn't go and the light turned green, because he was texting and had no clue the light had turned green; or when the person behind me honked at me because I was doing my makeup. Patience, please! What is more important than a straight lipstick line that you don't have time to do before leaving for work? I'm that girl.

*   When you felt rejected because you didn't get invited to the party. Of course, what comes next...the reel begins...feelings of inadequacy, head to toe. You don't measure up. You'll never be enough.

*   When our families feel more like a war zone than a safe haven, arguing over stupid stuff we won't even remember in a few days. Anybody relate?

*   When loss hits hard and you're not sure you can love again. Loss leaves us in such agony and pain at times, it's hard to think straight much less function well. Staying in bed for days on end can seem like the best option, but it isn't the loving option for anyone.

You get the picture. Life happens; and when it does over and over again on any given day, leaving us feeling hopeless, confused, and alone, how can we get really good at setting our default to Love Anyway? That's exactly what God's plan for us is: to literally default to *Love Anyway!*

Here's what I mean....

❝1 Corinthians 13:4-8 NASB

4 Love is patient, love is kind and is not jealous; love does not brag and is not arrogant, **5** does not act unbecomingly; it does not seek its own, is not provoked, does not take into account a wrong suffered, **6** does not rejoice in unrighteousness, but rejoices with the truth; **7** bears all things, believes all things, hopes all things, endures all things. **8** *love never fails*. ❞

I double-dog dare you to try something for the next 21 days! Read that passage and put your name in place of love and attach faith to it, which makes it a declaration over your life. Imagine this declaration being real and true of who you actually are. Believe God that love's characteristics will become yours! Go ahead now and put your name in place of "love" in these translations, too. You will love enjoying the effects of it in your life.

4 Love is large and incredibly patient. Love is gentle and consistently kind to all. It refuses to be jealous when blessing comes to someone else. Love does not brag about one's achievements nor inflate its own importance. 5 Love does not traffic in shame and disrespect, nor selfishly seek its own honor. Love is not easily irritated or quick to take offense. 6 Love joyfully celebrates honesty and finds no delight in what is wrong. 7 Love is a safe place of shelter, for it never stops believing the best for others. Love never takes failure as defeat, for it never gives up (TPT).

And I ♡ this one!

"Let me describe love. Love stays in difficult relationships with kindness. Love does not play 'oneupmanship,' nor does it react to those who do. Love is not rude or grasping or overly sensitive, nor does love search for imperfections and faults in others. Love is the most enduring quality of human existence. It keeps on keeping on; it trusts in God in every situation and expects God to act in all circumstances. Nothing can destroy love." (Johnson)

Want A Fail-Proof Life?

Quote this every morning and put your name everywhere it says love.

Love suffers long and is kind;

Love does not envy;

Love does not parade itself, is not puffed up;

Love does not behave rudely,

Love does not seek its own,

Love is not provoked,

Love thinks no evil;

Love does not rejoice in iniquity,

Love rejoices in the truth;

Love bears all things,

Love believes all things,

Love hopes all things,

Love endures all things.

Love never fails...

Love

God is Love

1 John 4:8

The love of God was poured out in our hearts by the Holy Spirit when we were born again according to Romans 5:5.

God's divine nature of love was deposited inside of you when you were born again. If you haven't been born again, pray this prayer right now and mean it with all of your heart.

Dear Lord,
Romans 10:13 says that whoever calls on the name of the Lord shall be saved. So I call on You now, Jesus, and repent of my sin. I choose to turn away from my old ways and walk in the light of Your Word now. I surrender my will to Yours and ask You to call the shots in my life from now on.
In Jesus' name I pray.
Amen.

Your life will never be the same once your heart is filled with the love of God! I cannot wait to hear from you! Please email me at ***hello@happyanyway.org*** and let me know you just accepted Christ as your Lord and Savior so I can help you take your next steps to grow as a believer! And let me be the first to congratulate you on the best decision of your life.

This is key whether you just prayed that prayer for the first time or maybe even simply took this opportunity to commit your heart afresh and anew to the Lord like I did as I wrote that prayer.

Proverbs says to:

Guard Your Heart

with all diligence for out of it flows the issues of life. Those forces of life are the fruit of the Spirit that flow out of love! They give life to us and to those around us. Have you ever heard "Garbage in, garbage out"? Well, that is what this verse is saying. Guard what goes into your heart so that life and not death will flow out of your heart. When the God kind of love that never fails flows out of our hearts, that is when we are truly living our best lives.

Get this!

There is no situation in life that at least one fruit of the Spirit won't come to your aid and help you overcome whatever it is you are facing.

I heard Gloria Copeland say that decades ago and it has stuck with me and proven to be absolutely true in my life.

So guess what that means?

When you feel like you can't wait any longer on the promise you are believing God for, tap into patience and that force of life will give you the power to keep on keeping on.

When you feel like you can't take rejection, loneliness or whatever has spiraled life out of control and you are so down that you wonder if you can go on any longer, yield to joy instead of sadness and you will find the strength to hold steady in the storm that rages in your soul. What does it look like to yield to the fruit of the Spirit? How to yield to the fruit of the Spirit is what the rest of this study is all about. No doubt, as you read the next pages of this devotional, answers you have been waiting for are going to become clear as to why relationships fall apart and how to love when we are heartbroken or even just irritated!

Get ready because I saved the best for last. I cannot wait to hear how this revolutionizes your life like it did mine!

Galatians 5:22-23 says that the fruit of the Spirit is love, joy, peace, patience, goodness, gentleness, faithfulness, kindness, and self-control.

Notice that it says the fruit of the Spirit is love....

"Is" is singular and what most scholars agree on is that the fruit of the Spirit is love and all of the other fruit flow out of love. This means that when we were born again, not only love but also joy, peace, patience, goodness, gentleness, faithfulness, kindness, and self-control were all poured out in our hearts.

The fruit of the Spirit are the very characteristics of God. It's as if God's DNA is deposited on the inside of us when we are born again. You could say God's personality is defined by the fruit of the Spirit. The word Christian means Christlike. Many people think it's all about trying to muster up enough willpower to behave well. Nooooo! Not at all. It's a supernatural work that is done in our hearts and our personality becomes more like God's personality when we bear the image of Christ.

Love makes a mark on us that can never be removed when we are born again. And when we follow hard after God, spending time with Him, abiding in His presence, our personalities begin to reflect His nature more and more. We walk out our lives making choices through the filter of love.

People think love is this mushy feeling we get when we watch a romantic comedy or when we kiss and the whole world seems to be set in order. Well, not exactly. Movies, music, and culture have us so confused about what love really is.

Have you ever noticed...

when we were born again, not only love but also joy, peace, patience, goodness, gentleness, faithfulness, kindness, and self-control were all poured out in our hearts!

Love is more like this:

* You are so mad that if you grit your teeth any harder, they just might break.

* You are so hurt that the pain is almost numbing and your heart is sick, broken, and despondent.

* You are so frustrated that you are overwhelmed and it paralyzes you.

* You are at a crossroads in each of these situations.

You can...

A. Throw a plate at your husband, which he dodges and it hits the wall and crashes. I heard of that happening once. (If you know me, you know this happened our first year of marriage. I tell you this so you can know that I have lived out the truths in this book and have experienced the change these truths can make! No more flying plates in my house! Glory be to God!)

B. Go to bed, pull the covers over your head and try to sleep the pain away. (Been there, done that, doesn't work.)

C. Give someone a piece of your mind and feel a little better after venting. (We've all done this I'm sure and could be part of why we are together in this book right now.)

Each of these options are called yielding to the flesh according to Romans 8.

OR...

You can...

A. Walk in the Spirit and yield to the fruit of the Spirit. But here's the catch. You will only be able to do this if you set your mind on the things of the Spirit rather than the things of the flesh according to Romans 8:5.

> **Romans 8:1 says,** "There is therefore now no condemnation to those who are in Christ Jesus, who do not walk according to the flesh, but according to the Spirit."

When we walk according to the Spirit in our lives, there is no condemnation, meaning we walk free from shame and blame that trip many of us up. The beautiful thing about this is that shame is so often the underlying cause of the evil we encounter and partake of. When we walk according to the Spirit, yielding to the fruit of the Spirit, we walk with righteousness, knowing who we are in Christ and not falling prey to shame, blame and insecurity. The flip side of this explains why we get super defensive when we know we are walking according to the flesh.

Shame, blame and deflecting our junk on others is what happens when there is condemnation from living life yielded to the flesh.

B. Abide in the Vine. John 15 tells us that the only way for us to really live is to abide in the presence of God. The idea is that God is the Vine and we are the branches; and just like with a real vine in nature, if a branch is cut off from the vine, its life source, it will die. In the same way, if we do not live connected to God and His ways of doing things, which are higher than ours, eventually areas of our lives will die. There will be pain, loss, and struggles that could be avoided. If we want to bear fruit in our lives and if we want the fruit of the Spirit to flow out of our lives with great force causing us to never fail, then we must stay connected to the Life-Source. There is no life apart from the Vine. Without connection, our actions bring forth death to relationships, opportunities, and even our health. But moments when we abide in the Vine, we are empowered by God to choose life in moments we are tempted to throw plates, become paralyzed with fear, or sink into depression.

c. Live life to the fullest! John 10:10 reveals that Jesus came to give us life and life more abundantly. The devil came to kill, steal and destroy. When we were born again, love came to dwell on the inside of us—all we have to do is stay in His Word, abide in Him, and His power will flow through us. If we are in the habit of yielding to anger, frustration, depression, or stress, it may have to be very deliberate at first, yielding to patience or gentleness instead of biting someone's head off or going off on someone. I am not talking about stuffing your emotions or repressing things. I am talking about a supernatural power called love that when yielded to causes you to win in life every time. *Note: our scoreboard may not be the same as God's, so I am not saying life will be a bed of roses.

Quite the contrary.

This is not a cotton-candy gospel. There is pain.

There is loss. There is challenge. We may not win

every battle. But we will win the war if we use the

greatest weapon available—

LOVE!

Love Never Fails!

1 CORINTHIANS 13:8

Love is...

Let's take a close look at each fruit of the Spirit and how they help us overcome any relational trouble we have experienced or will ever face.

Love is...the essence of who God is and the essence of what life is all about.

It's why we do everything we do. It's what we want more than anything else out of our existence, and it is the reason we were made—to love and be loved. God is love and when we believe in Him, we believe in Love. When we believe in love, we understand that even though the whole world is going crazy and has spun out of control, God is reaching in to save humanity through you and me to the degree that we will cooperate with Him. His love is inside of us if we are born-again believers and flows out of us creating a fail-proof life as we yield to love's powerful forces. Let's dive into what I mean by this.

Choose to love even when it is difficult to do so. It's the secret to a happy and fulfilled life!

Joy is...

Joy is...like a stream or a fountain.

If you have ever walked along the rocky bed of a beautiful, winding stream, you know that the water is so pure, you can drink from it. Joy can purify us and helps get the debris and garbage out that inevitably collects in our lives over time. I think of how a spring or fountain keeps water moving so that it doesn't become stagnant, stinky, and filled with yuck. Joy is like that in our lives as Isaiah 12:3 says, "With joy you will draw water from the springs of salvation" (Berean Study Bible). Again Psalm 87:7 says, "...all my springs of joy are in you" (NASB).

So this is how joy strengthens us, as Nehemiah 8:10 says, when we choose to yield to joy. Joy cleanses our hearts from the stress and sadness that tries to dog our tracks. How awesome is that?! Next time you are tempted to throw a pity party for yourself or pull the covers over your head in despair, instead think—SPA DAY! And grab some joy from the springs of salvation that are inside of you, ready to help you overcome and filter out whatever is overwhelming you at the moment!

> So repent [change your inner self—your old way of thinking, regret past sins] and return [to God—seek His purpose for your life], so that your sins may be wiped away [blotted out, completely erased], so that times of refreshing may come from the presence of the Lord [restoring you like a cool wind on a hot day] (Acts 3:19 AMP).

A crystal-clear bubbling brook is so refreshing on a hot summer's day. I grew up in Mississippi and we would ride horses through a 100-acre forest from daylight to to sunset all summer long as kids. We knew where the streams were and I remember cupping my hands and drinking water from certain places that were clean. When we go into His presence, we come out refreshed and filled with joy much like sipping from those streams on sunny days in the Mississippi heat.

Joy is...

A merry heart does good like medicine the Word tells us. So joy is literally connected to our health. Medical science has proven that happy people (optimists) live longer. When we find ourselves down in the dumps and stir up the joy inside of us, we improve our health.

When I began to see joy this way, the imagery in my mind helped me see how powerful joy is and actually understand how it works in our hearts.

There is a lot more on joy and "how to happy" in my first book called *Happy ANYWAY*. It is the story of how I overcame depression and is truly a road map that could lead you to new levels of joy in your life.

What is something you are going through that could just zap your joy if you let it? Take a moment in His presence right now. Cry out to God and let Him strengthen you. Jot down a few nuggets of wisdom He speaks to you regarding your situation that will bring you strength in the coming days. Ask Him to speak to you. He will.

_____

_____

_____

_____

_____

_____

_____

_____

Choose joy and experience strength to get through whatever it is you are up against.

Peace is...

Peace is...like an umpire between our soul and our spirit. (See Colossians 3:15.)

When we are trying to make a decision, Hebrews 12:14 tells us to follow peace. Peace in our hearts is the guide that will never lead us astray from the plan of God for our lives. Even if our minds and flesh are pulling us one way, peace will pull us Yahweh, if we yield to it! When we do, things work out soooo much better.

Can you think of a decision you have made when you did follow peace and what was the outcome?

_____

_____

What about a decision where you didn't follow peace? What was the outcome?

_____

_____

Is there a decision you are trying to make now that you need wisdom about? Try this: Imagine making the decision going one direction and check in your spirit. Is there peace? Now imagine making a different decision regarding that situation. Which one brings peace to your heart? It may not even make sense to your head but if you are full of the Word of God and your heart is tuned into God, your heart will lead you in the best direction.

What brings you peace when you imagine going this way or that?

_____

_____

Choose peace and you will make wise decisions that will take you where God is leading you!

Patience is...

Patience is...there!

We've all heard people say, "Don't pray for patience because then God will give you a reason to need it!" Ha! Or we have heard people say, "I just don't have the patience for that!"

Actually neither is true. You do have patience. It is inside of you if you are born again just like all the other fruit. Now it's just a matter of learning how to grow patience which is actually done by yielding to it. James 1:2-8 says,

> **2** My brethren, count it all joy when you fall into various trials, **3** knowing that the testing of your faith produces patience. **4** But let patience have its perfect work, that you may be perfect and complete, lacking nothing. **5** If any of you lacks wisdom, let him ask of God, who gives to all liberally and without reproach, and it will be given to him. **6** But let him ask in faith, with no doubting, for he who doubts is like a wave of the sea driven and tossed by the wind. **7** For let not that man suppose that he will receive anything from the Lord; **8** he is a double-minded man, unstable in all his ways.

Let patience have its perfect work. How? So often we run from pain and trouble. Embrace it, face it, and place it in the hands of our loving Father. Patience is the powerful force that helps us be able to do this.

It has been said that faith and patience are the power twins. We want things to happen for us and work out for us in our favor. The problem is that we want them NOW! And it takes faith and patience working together to trust in the Lord for our desperate situations to turn around like we so need them to.

Why are you in need of patience right now? Ask God to help you yield to patience and faith and write down what that will look like for you.

_____

_____

Patience is...

What outcome are you believing Him for and is that the outcome you believe God wants for you?

_____

_____

Think about it this way. When we order something online and hit the final purchase button, we throw our hands up in glee and shout, "Woohoo!" As far as we are concerned that new pair of shoes or whatever is ours! We go and tell people if we are super excited about it. And we tell people we have a new _____! But it hasn't even shown up yet. Why are we so sure it is ours? Because we paid for it and have the receipt, right? Well, that is why we can be so sure that what we pray for is ours as long as it is in line with the will of God. He tells us that if we ask anything according to His will, it is done for us. When we are connected to His heart and ask for things to help us live the lives He has called us to live, and that we desire, He is the God who keeps His promises to us. We can rest in faith, patiently waiting for Him to deliver to us what Jesus paid for on the cross. Jesus paid the ultimate price for our salvation. It includes eternal salvation but it also includes all the saving we require throughout our lives too.

Let's pray together now for your needs. I encourage you to write down this prayer of faith yielding to patience just like when you order something knowing it's coming but just not overnight!

_____

_____

Choose patience and you will hold steady in the storm and not waver, trusting God to see you through to the promise.

Kindness is...

Kindness is...calm power knowing who really is in control.

We all know people who try to dominate. We may be one of those people. We jokingly cope with our rudeness by saying we are "control freaks" or we manipulate the whole idea to seem like it is someone else's fault when sparks fly. Sound familiar?

If you have a hot temper, a blunt way of saying things, and a need for control, to blame, or to shame your every move, this could be the fruit to focus on. This fruit is one I have really worked on developing over the years and have found life just goes better when we yield to kindness. With kindness comes a gracious spirit about us rather than a rigid harsh way.

We might say something set us off so much so that it felt like something came all over us and we were "madder than a hatter"? Guess what? Something did come all over us! It's called an evil spirit. The spirit realm is real.

" Ephesians 6:12 (KJV)

For we wrestle not against flesh and blood, but against principalities, against powers, against the rulers of the darkness of this world, against spiritual wickedness in high places.**"**

So basically what this means is we have a choice to make when we get angry, want to speak harshly or be sharp in our tone with people. We can yield to true power that is found in kindness or we can yield to evil spirits that "come all over us" in anger, bitterness, and strife. Which one do you think will yield the life we want?

We are commanded in scripture to be kind. The great news is we reap what we sow. Want to reap kindness? Then spread it around like confetti.

❝Ephesians 4:32 (TPT)

But instead be kind and affectionate toward one another. Has God graciously forgiven you? Then graciously forgive one another in the depths of Christ's love.❞

Who is someone that is hard to be kind to and why?

_____

_____

_____

_____

How can what we just studied together help you be kind going forward?

_____

_____

_____

_____

_____

Choose kindness and enjoy the calm that comes with knowing that when you sow kindness, you will attract gracious treatment from others.

Goodness is...Love in action!

Love's action that causes our faith to work is goodness.

Faith without works is dead. There are three verses in James chapter 2 that say this! So that to me pretty much says in all caps "FAITH WITHOUT WORKS IS DEAD!" I love the way this passage frames goodness. Clearly it is not saying we are saved by works. We are certainly saved by grace and not by works.

I love the part that says, "show me your faith without works and I will show you my faith by my works." This is NOT about "trying to be good." Not at all! It is about being so in love with Jesus, we not only give lip service but we back up our faith with action. We are not human doings but rather human beings. Part of being who we are as Christians simply results in doing good. Goodness just becomes part of who we are. It's a by-product of faith in Christ. When we let the goodness of God flow out of us, it will draw people to the love of God in us.

Lester Sumrall said, "Goodness is love in its noblest form of behavior in society. It is holiness put into practice and not on dress parade." This makes me think of the verse in 2 Timothy 3:5 that says, "Having a form of godliness but denying its power. And from such people turn away!"

God has goodwill toward men and we are to be imitators of Him. That means we are to have goodwill toward men.

The Bible says it's the goodness of God that brings people to repentance. So this kind of goodness is powerful and has saving grace within it! Jesus also went about preaching the gospel and doing good. Part of the good He did was healing the sick and raising the dead. So goodness isn't just being passive and nice and letting people run over you; but actively doing good involves the very power of God. The good God has called us to do could actually carry healing power in it. You never know who is waiting on the other side of your obedience, so do the good God is leading you to do for someone!

Goodness is...

When I think of love in action, I think of Lisa Young. She was a guest speaker at Happy Girl Conference, and a few weeks prior to her coming, she texted me, asking for my address. I assumed this was to send books and things, but a few days later a package arrived in the mail with the cutest sweater she had gotten for me and the most encouraging little note. What she didn't know is that I was so discouraged at that point with the many obstacles that we were encountering as we prepared for the conference. I was wishing I could back out, sit down, give up, and quit. I knew I couldn't but that note and gift literally was the goodness of God expressed through a friend who yielded to the fruit of the Spirit. That one act of goodness was like fuel for me and literally put courage into me that sustained me up to the conference. It put just the pep in my step I needed to help me lead our amazing team, who pulled off the most fruitful conference we have had to date! Never underestimate the power of goodness that can be shared with a friend or family member or even a stranger as the Spirit leads.

What is something good God is leading you to do for someone that would bring encouragement for them?

_____

_____

List some times God has used you like this to show goodness to someone or when someone has shown goodness to you and the results of it:

_____

_____

Choose goodness and live a life of showing God's love in meaningful ways that will draw people to you.

Faithfulness is...summed up by swearing to your own hurt and changing not. (Psalm 15:4)

> an unfaithful man in time of trouble is like a bad tooth and a foot out of joint (Proverbs 25:19).

We don't want to be that to anyone do we? The way to be faithful is to yield to this part of God's divine nature that we have been given. We were given a measure of faith (faithfulness) and as we yield to it, the more faithful we become.

One of the biggest ways we can be faithful is in what we share and don't share about others' struggles. If we control our mouth, we control our whole body.

❝Proverbs 11:13

A talebearer reveals secrets, but he who is of a faithful spirit conceals a matter.❞

❝Matthew 25:21

His lord said to him, 'Well done, good and faithful servant; you were faithful over a few things, I will make you ruler over many things. Enter into the joy of your lord.'❞

These are the words we all hope to hear. In reality, though, this is a fruit of the Spirit that must be developed in order for us to hear these words. That's a sobering thought. The good news is that His mercies are new every morning and again, this is not a matter of willpower. It is leaning into the grace of God that is there for the getting and staying vitally connected to the Vine, as in John 15, which we discussed earlier.

Faithfulness is...

God is faithful and the more we stay connected to Him, the more faithful we become.

In what ways are you faithful?

_____

_____

_____

_____

What are the areas of faithfulness you struggle with?

_____

_____

_____

_____

What is something going on in your life that you really want to quit on, not show up for, or be done with, but you know it's just a difficult season and you need to dig deep and be faithful?

_____

_____

_____

_____

Choose faithfulness and you will excel and be promoted beyond your wildest dreams!

Gentleness is...

Gentleness is...others-minded, courteous, tender, and soft.

> For a true servant of our Lord Jesus will not be argumentative but gentle toward all and skilled in helping others see the truth, having great patience toward the immature (2 Timothy 2:24 TPT).

It's really neat to see how gentleness and patience work together in order to have great people skills. It appears here that gentleness helps us be able to have patience with people who are immature. Ahhhhh, got it! Gentleness could really come in handy for all those people who honk at me or ride with me when I drive. And my husband said, "Amen!"

Sidenote: I did hit a school bus once, a big yellow school bus. Yep, and little did I know at 16 years old that one of those kids on the bus would end up being my brother-in-law and remind me of this every holiday we are together.

Seriously though, think of someone you know who is gentle with you even when you mess up royally, even if you run into a big yellow school bus! This person is likely merciful and patient with you. I think of several people I know like this and at the top of the list is my husband. I can be a pill. He says he thinks I am half Greek. I'm loud, silly and pretty much say it like it is. Gentleness is something I so admire in others and attempt to yield to it as a habit as well, which helps to offset the passionate part of me that otherwise can be too harsh and brash.

I often remind myself of this verse, and when you make this a go-to verse for you, it can also take the edge off for you like it does me.

> **28** Come to me, all you who are weary and burdened, and I will give you rest. **29** Take my yoke upon you and learn from me, for I am gentle and humble in heart, and you will find rest for your souls. **30** For my yoke is easy and my burden is light (Matthew 11:28-30 NIV).

His yoke is easy and when we come to Him with our stress and anxiety, we learn gentleness and humility, as they typically go hand in hand; and we leave His presence with a lightheartedness about us. When we are stressed, it is an outward evidence that we are not coming to Him, and learning of Him, and finding rest in Him. I've noticed that people who are genuinely not stressed out all the time are also people who are regularly finding rest for their souls in His presence.

Gentleness knows you can afford to walk in love in any situation rather than getting stressed or uptight about things. Gentleness exudes patience and kindness toward people who are immature. Gentleness is a powerful force that can help you navigate all kinds of difficulties and come out on top.

Don't you just love people who are gentle? Gentle people have a way of making you feel so loved and safe. I want to be this way for others. I love how the Holy Spirit is a gentleman and how God doesn't force Himself on anyone but rather gently nudges us toward the light so we can take refuge away from the darkness. Have you ever noticed that gently nudging people usually works so much better than trying to overpower and control them?

Can you think of a person who has a gentle personality?

_____

What is it about them you enjoy and could learn from?

_____

Can you think of a time that, had you responded with gentleness, the outcome of a conversation could have been different?
What did you say?

_____

What would gentleness have said?

_____

Choose gentleness which is fostered by rest and humility. You will notice that as you do, stress and anxiety will fall off of you.

Self-control is...like the bookend to all the other fruits.

Self-control is needed in order to yield to any of the fruit of the Spirit. Think about how smart God is. He placed all of these powerful forces inside of us and then turbocharged them with what is like oil in the engine, so all the rest of the fruit of the Spirit flows out of us more easily and creates the life we all long for! That turbocharge which is like the secret sauce to loving ANYWAY, is self-control. All we have to do is yield to it!

Pressure off of us and onto Him! How liberating is that?!

Here's how this works:

❝1 Peter 5:5-11

5 Likewise you younger people, submit yourselves to your elders. Yes, all of you be submissive to one another, and be clothed with humility, for "God resists the proud, but gives grace to the humble." **6** Therefore humble yourselves under the mighty hand of God, that He may exalt you in due time, **7** casting all your care upon Him, for He cares for you. **8** Be sober, be vigilant; because your adversary the devil walks about like a roaring lion, seeking whom he may devour. **9** Resist him, steadfast in the faith, knowing that the same sufferings are experienced by your brotherhood in the world. **10** But may the God of all grace, who called us to His eternal glory by Christ Jesus, after you have suffered a while, perfect, establish, strengthen, and settle you. **11** To Him be the glory and the dominion forever and ever. Amen.❞

Self-Control is...

Step one:

Submit our hearts fully to God. When we submit to God, new levels of humility are created in the areas where we are submitted.

I believe this changes our very mindset about things; as we think in our hearts so are we.

Step two:

Yield to self-control or else life can spin completely out of control! We often want to control everything but ourselves! This passage shows us that there has to be an act of our will to resist the devil and when we do, he simply flees. But there is a progression and a process that will make this work or not work. The devil is seeking whom he may devour; so when he knocks and says, "May I come in?" the way to say, "No!" is outlined in these two steps.

Then the results of this yielding to self-control are exactly what we all want in life:

One—God adds His grace to our self-control that enables us to accomplish and overcome what is before us.

Two—He perfects, establishes, strengthens, and settles us, which causes our lives to bring glory to Him in all we do.

One way He perfects, establishes, strengthens, and settles us is by instructing us in Ephesians 4:22-25 to daily put on the new man. We are commanded to put off the old man, which would include anger, aggression, and impatience. Yielding to self-control becomes second nature when we are in the habit of putting on our new nature. I literally pretended to put on an imaginary coat each morning as I quoted Ephesians 4:22-25 when I was in the beginning stages of learning to yield to the fruit of the Spirit. And still, on the mornings when I remember, I imagine, "putting on the new man," dressed in the Spirit for all that life will bring that day.

Self-Control is...

We are transformed by the renewing of our minds and below are some great verses that will renew your mind and strengthen you to be able to yield to self-control.

As you read them, note the areas of life where you need to exercise more self-control.

_____

_____

Titus 1:8 (TPT)

> He should be one who is known for his hospitality and a lover of goodness. He should be recognized as one who is fair-minded, pure-hearted, and self-controlled.

Proverbs 25:28 (TPT)

> If you live without restraint and are unable to control your temper, you're as helpless as a city with broken-down defenses, open to attack.

Philippians 2:4 (TPT)

> Abandon every display of selfishness. Possess a greater concern for what matters to others instead of your own interests.

1 Peter 4:7 (TPT)

> Since we are approaching the end of all things, be intentional, purposeful, and self-controlled so that you can be given to prayer.

Self-Control is...

"Luke 21:34-36 (TPT)

34 Be careful that you never allow your hearts to grow cold. Remain passionate and free from anxiety and the worries of this life. Then you will not be caught off guard by what happens. Don't let me come and find you drunk or careless in living like everyone else. **35** For that day will come as a shocking surprise to all, like a downpour that drenches everyone, catching many unaware and un-prepared. **36** Keep a constant watch over your soul, and pray for the courage and grace to prevail over these things that are destined to occur and that you will stand before the presence of the Son of Man with a clear conscience.**"**

Are you seeing just how true it is that there will never be any situation that you will face life in which at least one of the fruit of the Spirit won't come to your aid and help you overcome?!

This is how love never fails! And this is how YOU can live a fail-proof life!

A REAL FRIEND IS
SOMEONE WHO
KNOWS
all about you
&
*LOVES
YOU*
anyway

*L*ove note from Heaven:

....

....

....

*O*bservation:

....

....

....

*V*ow:

....

....

....

*E*xamining my ♥ in prayer:

....

....

....

*L*ove note from Heaven:

....

....

....

*O*bservation:

....

....

....

*V*ow:

....

....

....

*E*xamining my ♥ in prayer:

....

....

....

$\mathcal{L}$ove note from Heaven:

· ·

· ·

· ·

$\mathcal{O}$bservation:

· ·

· ·

· ·

$\mathcal{V}$ow:

· ·

· ·

· ·

$\mathcal{E}$xamining my ♥ in prayer:

· ·

· ·

· ·

*L*ove note from Heaven:

....

....

....

*O*bservation:

....

....

....

*V*ow:

....

....

....

*E*xamining my ♥ in prayer:

....

....

....

• THINK ABOUT •

TOOTY FRUITY

Rank the fruit of the Spirit that are most abundant in your life:

....

....

....

....

....

....

....

What will you do to focus on the fruit you need to yield to more?

....

....

....

....

....

....

....

....

....

Fruit of the Spirit:

LOVE · JOY · PEACE · PATIENCE · KINDNESS · GOODNESS · FAITHFULNESS · GENTLENESS · SELF-CONTROL

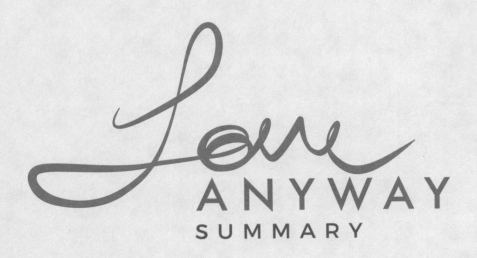

ANYWAY

SUMMARY

1. God is Love + Love is real = God is real!

2. God is good + The devil is bad = God works all things together for good.

3. Love God + Love yourself = Love others well

4. God's love for us + A world gone crazy = Faith beyond our understanding

5. Forgiveness > Bitterness, pain, and suffering

6. Love ANYWAY = A happy and fulfilled life by yielding to the fruit of the Spirit

We may not win every battle. But we will win the war if we use the greatest weapon available—L O V E !

ADRIENNE COOLEY

When we *Love* **ANYWAY, that hole in our heart is filled with His love.**

Notice that you can still see the puzzle pieces. Similarly there may be scars but we can truly be made whole again by His great love! When we bring God our broken hearts, He mends them and gives us the happy and fulfilled life we desire!

I hope you have enjoyed reading *Love* ANYWAY as much as I enjoyed writing it! I put my whole heart into it.

Want MORE?

You can also get *happy* ANYWAY on Amazon or at my website at adriennecooley.com

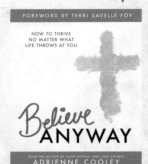

Believe ANYWAY is coming soon and will also be available on Amazon or at adriennecooley.com and in bookstores everywhere!

The *Love* ANYWAY Online Course is available at adriennecooley.com. I created this to be a *next step* for you in addition to the book. The content is different but digs in a little deeper in some ways plus there is a private FACEBOOK Group and a community you can join that will help change the landscape of your relationships and take them to a whole new level!

- ✶ Eight 20-30 minute video modules
- ✶ Printable worksheets
- ✶ Actionable challenges to help create change
- ✶ Complete audio version
- ✶ Full manuscript of each module
- ✶ Bonus videos
- ✶ and more

HAPPY GIRL CONFERENCE is a conference I host and am so thankful to have amazing speakers each year like Lisa Young, Terri Savelle Foy, Pattie Duininck, Peppi Sims and others. God always sends just the right message to spread the happy, share the love, and spark purpose in the lives of those who join the fun!

I hope you will join us this upcoming year. You can find out the details at adriennecooley.com and subscribe to my #HappyMondayBlog there, too!

See you in your inbox!

Follow me on social media so we can stay connected!
Facebook: Adrienne Cooley
Instagram & Twitter: @addiecooley